Sweet Smell of Success

Music by Marvin Hamlisch
Lyrics by Craig Carnelia
Book by John Guare

Cover Photos: Paul Kolnik

Original Cast Recording Available on Sony Classical

ISBN 0-634-04935-6

HAL•LEONARD®
CORPORATION
7777 W. BLUEMOUND RD. P.O. BOX 13819 MILWAUKEE, WI 53213

In Australia Contact:
Hal Leonard Australia Pty. Ltd.
22 Taunton Drive P.O. Box 5130
Cheltenham East, 3192 Victoria, Australia
Email: ausadmin@halleonard.com

Visit Hal Leonard Online at
www.halleonard.com

Craig Carnelia has written two shows to date with Marvin Hamlisch. The first, *Sweet Smell of Success*, opened on Broadway in March 2002, receiving both Drama Desk and Tony Award nominations for Best Score. In December 2002, the team followed up this debut with their second Broadway offering, the score for Nora Ephron's play with music, *Imaginary Friends*. As both composer and lyricist, Craig wrote the score for the Broadway musical *Is There Life After High School?* and contributed four songs to Studs Terkel's *Working,* for which he received his first Tony nomination. Off-Broadway, he wrote music and lyrics for *Three Postcards* at Playwrights Horizons and contributed single songs to *The No-Frills Revue, Diamonds* and *A...My Name Is Still Alice*. There are two critically acclaimed compilation recordings of his songs: *Pictures in the Hall* and *Cast of Thousands*, as well as a published collection of his works entitled *The Songs of Craig Carnelia*.

As a composer, **Marvin Hamlisch** has won virtually every major award that exists: three Oscars, four Grammys, four Emmys, a Tony and three Golden Globe awards; his groundbreaking show, *A Chorus Line*, received the Pulitzer Prize. Among the Broadway shows Hamlisch has composed are *They're Playing Our Song, The Goodbye Girl, Sweet Smell of Success* and *Imaginary Friends*. He is the composer of more than forty motion picture scores, including his Oscar-winning score and song for *The Way We Were* and his adaptation of Scott Joplin's music for *The Sting*, for which he received his third Oscar. His prolific output of scores for films include original compositions and/or musical adaptations for *Sophie's Choice, Ordinary People, The Swimmer, Three Men and a Baby, Ice Castles, Take the Money and Run, Bananas* and *Save the Tiger*. Mr. Hamlisch was Musical Director and arranger for Barbra Streisand's 1994 concert tour of the U.S. and England, as well as the television special, "Barbra Streisand: The Concert" (for which he received two of his Emmys). He served in the same capacities for her Millennium concerts.

Contents

6	I Cannot Hear the City
10	Welcome to the Night
16	Laughin' All the Way to the Bank
21	At the Fountain
31	Don't Know Where You Leave Off
40	For Susan
49	One Track Mind
56	Rita's Tune
62	Dirt
67	Don't Look Now
75	At the Fountain (Reprise)

John Lithgow

Brian D'Arcy Jam

From left to right: Marvin Hamlisch, Brian D'Arcy Jam
John Guare, Craig Carnelia, John Lithg

John Lithgow and Cast

Brian D'Arcy James

Kelli O'Hara and
Jack Noseworthy

Front Cover photos, clockwise from the top:

- David Brummel, John Lithgow and
  Brian D'Arcy James

- Brian D'Arcy James and John Lithgow

- Eric Michael Gillett, Brian D'Arcy James
  and Stacey Logan

- Michelle Kittrell and Jennie Ford

- Kelli O'Hara and Jack Noseworthy

- Brian D'Arcy James and Eric Michael Gillett

Photos: Paul Kolnik

I CANNOT HEAR THE CITY

Music by MARVIN HAMLISCH
Lyrics by CRAIG CARNELIA

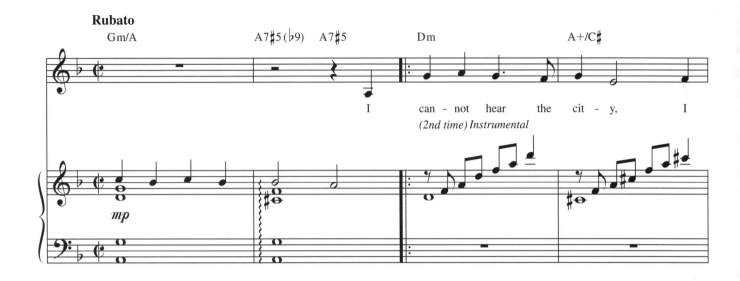

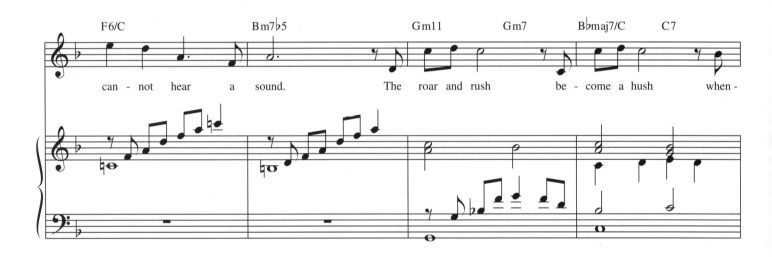

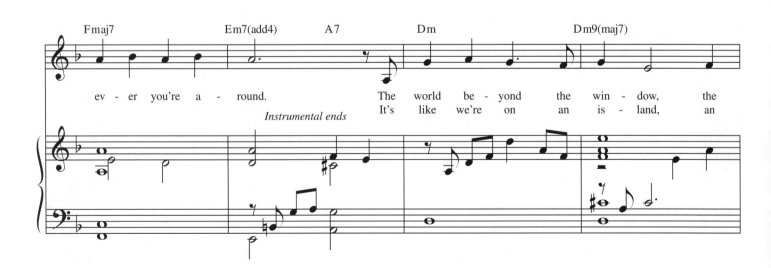

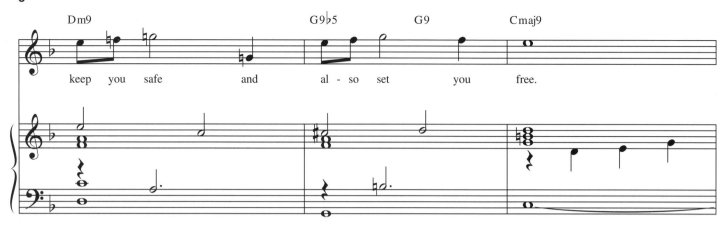

keep you safe and al - so set you free.

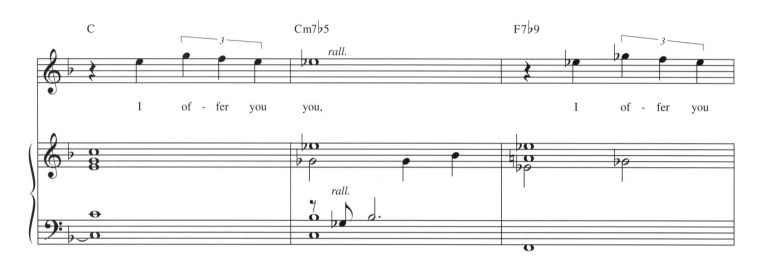

I of - fer you you, I of - fer you

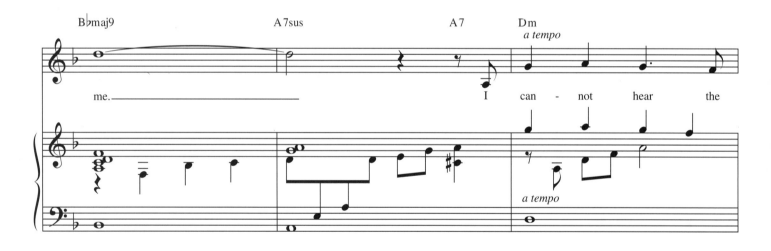

me._____ I can - not hear the

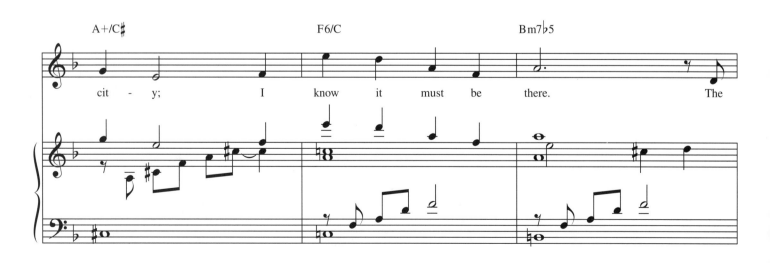

cit - y; I know it must be there. The

WELCOME TO THE NIGHT

Music by MARVIN HAMLISCH
Lyrics by CRAIG CARNELIA

LAUGHIN' ALL THE WAY
TO THE BANK

Music by MARVIN HAMLISCH
Lyrics by CRAIG CARNELIA

Quickly, in 2

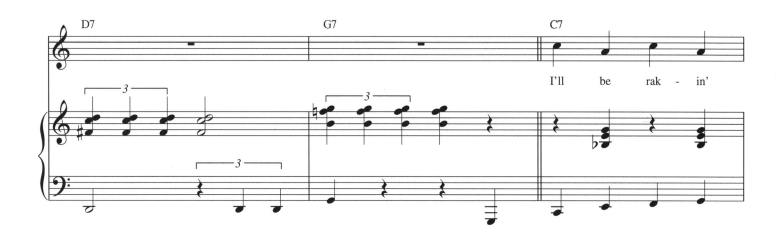

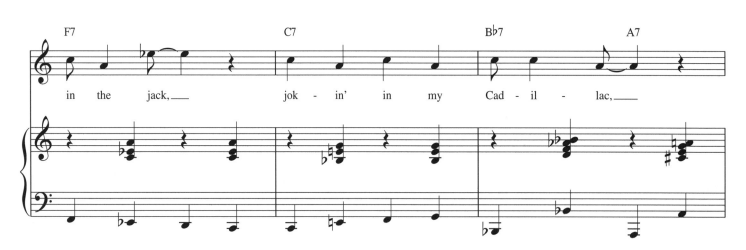

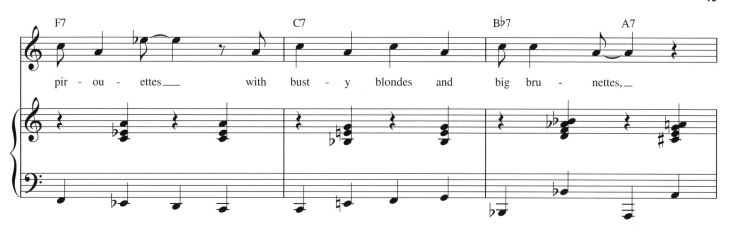

pir - ou - ettes___ with bust - y blondes and big bru - nettes, __

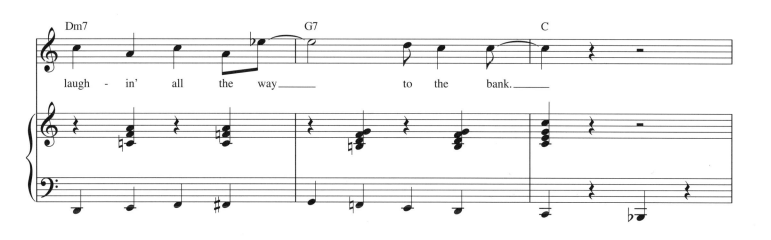

laugh - in' all the way_____ to the bank._____

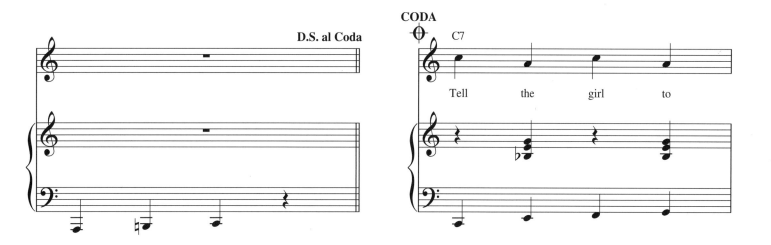

D.S. al Coda

CODA

C7

Tell the girl to

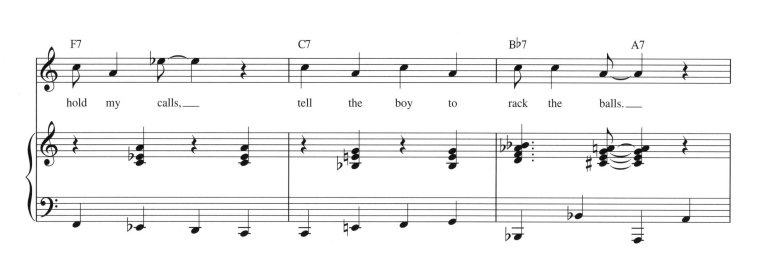

hold my calls, __ tell the boy to rack the balls. __

Laugh - in' all the way,_____ laugh - in' all the way,___

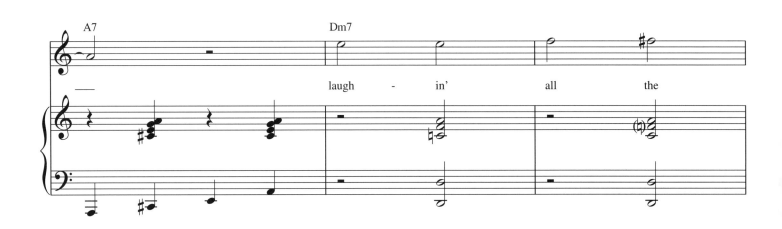

_____ laugh - in' all the

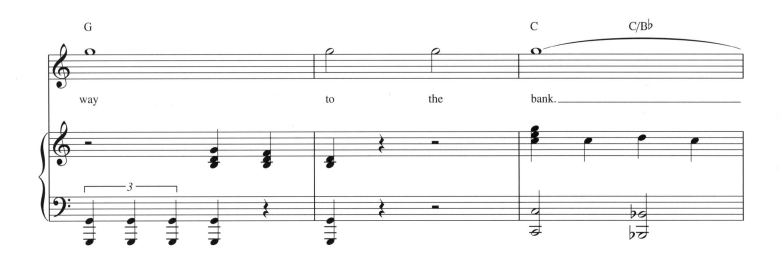

way to the bank._____

AT THE FOUNTAIN

Music by MARVIN HAMLISCH
Lyrics by CRAIG CARNELIA

gin? Fal - co - ne might_ just win._____

So man - y times you thought the way was clear,_____

on - ly to find you can't get there from here._____ Here's your

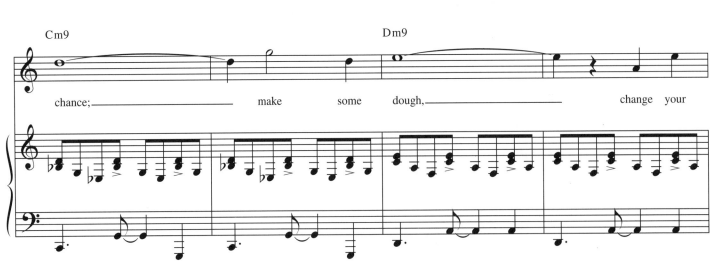

chance;_____ make some dough,_____ change your

Am/C   Dm9

a way with a word,_____ quick with a joke___

Cmaj7   N.C.

we've al-read-y heard.___ *"Y'ever hear the one about Lana Turner?* *Sittin' at the soda fountain...*

Slow — eerily, dreamy

Bmaj7   G#9

dreamin' her soda fountain dreams..." But there was some - thing he could see_____ for just a

(ad lib arps.)

D#m9   G#9   Bmaj7   C#9

mo - ment;___ it's like he saw___ in-side of me what's real-ly

_∧ *sim.*

DON'T KNOW WHERE YOU LEAVE OFF

Music by MARVIN HAMLISCH
Lyrics by CRAIG CARNELIA

Moderately, flowing

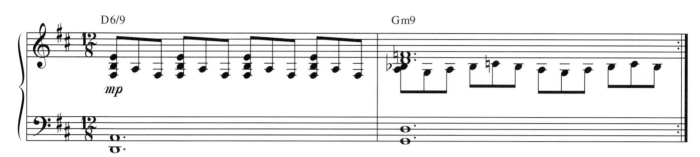

DALLAS

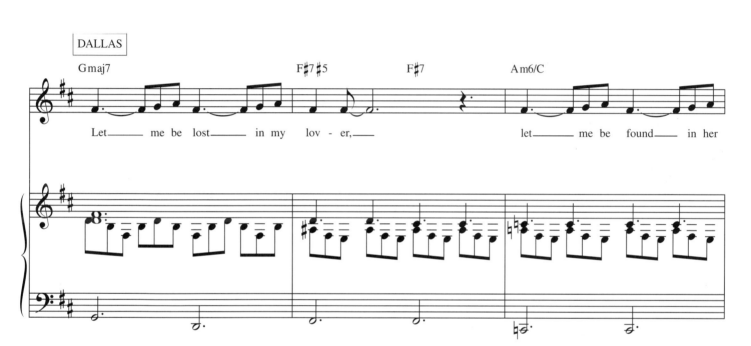

Let me be lost in my lov-er, let me be found in her

eyes, Su-san. Let me keep com-in' back to where I've just

FOR SUSAN

Music by MARVIN HAMLISCH
Lyrics by CRAIG CARNELIA

Flowing, in one

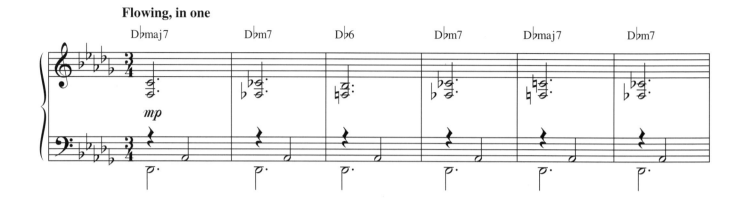

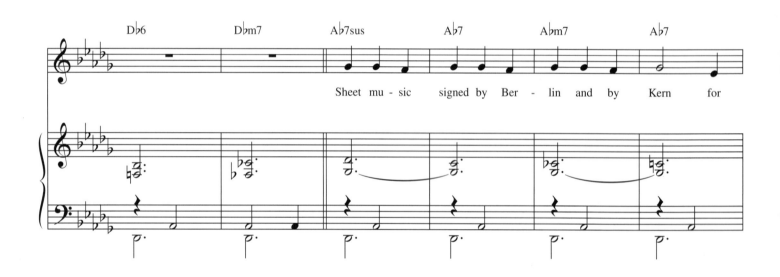

Sheet mu-sic signed by Ber-lin and by Kern for

Su-san._____ Bo-gie sends "Buck-ets of

Some-one has changed her, some-one all wrong for Su - san.

There's some-one, some school-boy,

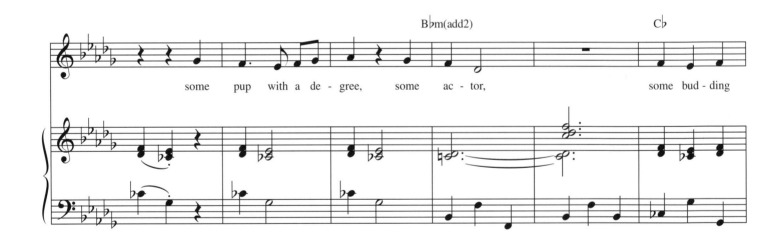

some pup with a de-gree, some ac-tor, some bud-ding

Bran - do mum-bling his lines for Su - san.

ONE TRACK MIND

Music by MARVIN HAMLISCH
Lyrics by CRAIG CARNELIA

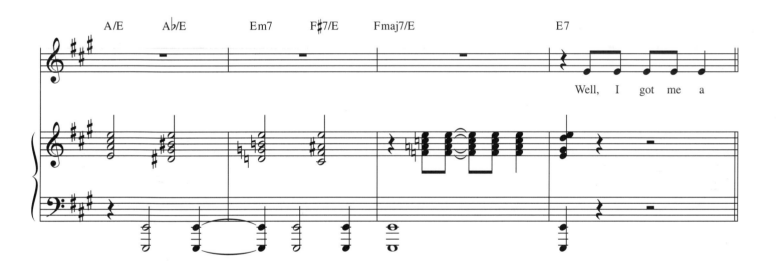

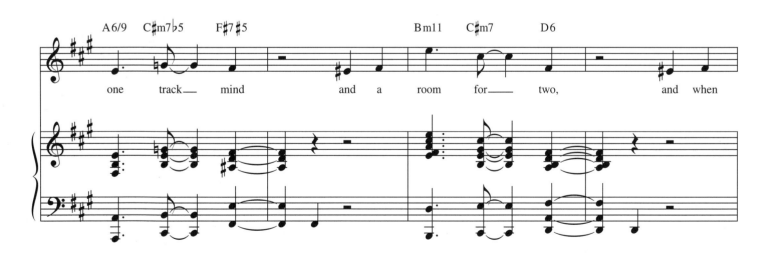

RITA'S TUNE

Music by MARVIN HAMLISCH
Lyrics by CRAIG CARNELIA

DIRT

Music by MARVIN HAMLISCH
Lyrics by CRAIG CARNELIA

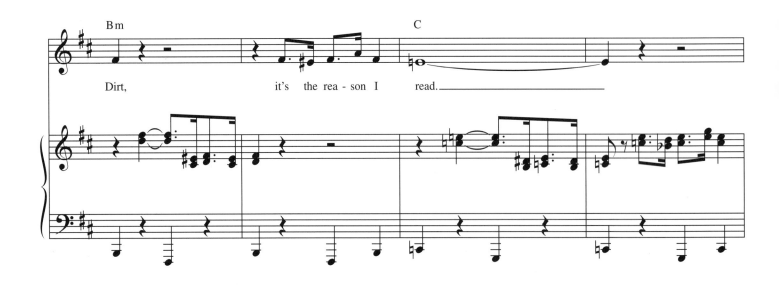

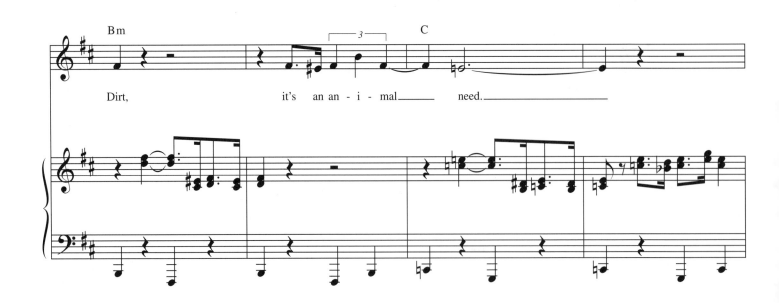

DON'T LOOK NOW

Music by MARVIN HAMLISCH
Lyrics by CRAIG CARNELIA

Freely, ad lib.

Ma-gi-cians al-ways tell you they've got noth-ing up their sleeve, but

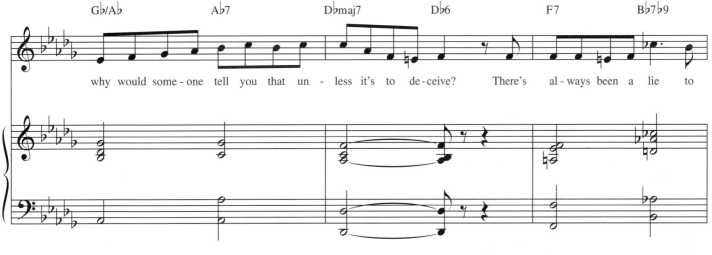

why would some-one tell you that un-less it's to de-ceive? There's al-ways been a lie to

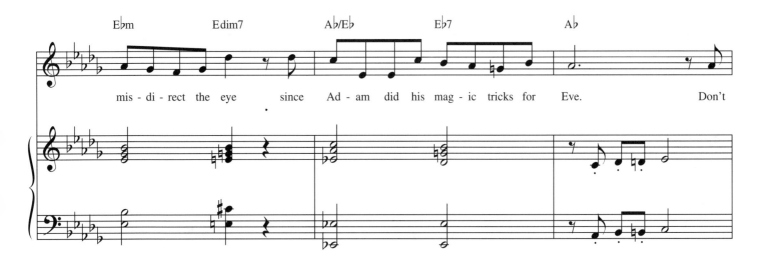

mis-di-rect the eye since Ad-am did his mag-ic tricks for Eve. Don't

took you to the clean-ers, don't you know? *(whistle)*

He walked you like a dog, the so and so.___ So,

say, "Bow Wow." A piece of what you had is

gone. The mag-ic act goes on and on.___ You're

AT THE FOUNTAIN
(Reprise)

Music by MARVIN HAMLISCH
Lyrics by CRAIG CARNELIA

Gently

fi - nal - ly at the foun - tain,

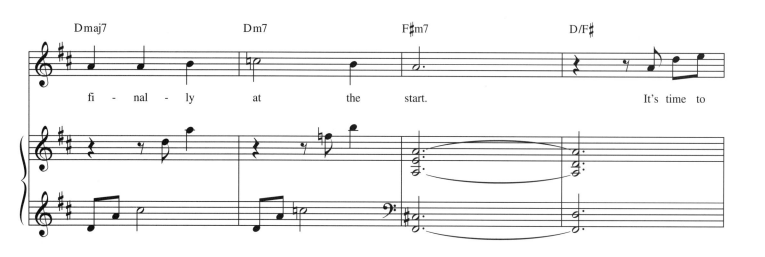

fi - nal - ly at the start. It's time to